My Heart is a Moth in a Glass Jar

Siyuan Carter-Patkau

My Heart is a Moth in a Glass Jar © 2022
Siyuan Carter-Patkau

All rights reserved.

No part of this publication may be reproduced, stored in a retrieval system, or transmitted, in any form or by any means, electronic, mechanical, photocopying, recording or otherwise, without the prior written permission of the presenters.

Siyuan Carter-Patkau asserts the moral right to be identified as author of this work.

Presentation by *BookLeaf Publishing*

Web: www.bookleafpub.com

E-mail: info@bookleafpub.com

ISBN: 978-93-95784-60-3

First edition 2022

DEDICATION

To my parents, friends, and teachers. Love always to you all.

PREFACE

Content warning: This collection contains references to sensitive subjects including eating disorders and sexual assault.

Penny for your Thoughts

I want for many things that
will never come to pass, like
the missing of someone who
is already gone. I
dropped pennies in a fountain,
day after day,
and watched the seasons change;
a forest sprang from the bed of copper, but
my wish stayed locked within its roots,
despite all my faith in superstition. (When
I dug up the floorboards, I found
a cache of someone else's
discarded dreams piling up like trash.)
One day, I will visit the graveyard where all
the shooting stars land, but
for now, I will lay in my hope-made bed
and toss another penny for posterity.

The Phantom Commune

I am a child playing jacks in a train station,
hiding from the sun in the platform's overhang,
silhouetted in the dark by the
ticket booth candle that never goes out.
The trains come and go, but
I am never quite right for them, and
the hush that falls when I board
sways me from settling.
No souls meet me in my in-between, though
I know they are there, spectres
lost in their own diversions.
If I were a little less of everything,
I might be a little more suited to something.

Lost in Translation

Did you ever receive my postcard?
I stuck on the stamp with super glue,
a superfluous measure that reminded me of you
and your neuroses that held such unwitting charm.
I missed your call by five minutes, and
I missed you when I purged my closet of fake IDs,
the cloak you gave me hiding in the back,
the faded fabric now fragile as glass.
What a morass I swim through.

Hunger Makes Me

I keep my hunger at bay through
a strict diet of submission,
following in the footsteps of those
bigger than myself, like playing
stepping stones, or hopscotch.

My hunger sits at the base of my throat,
a pulsing egg ready to hatch,
words riper than a tomato in October,
eager to spill forth in the form of
something like an opinion,
bile I must constantly swallow
in pursuit of perfection.

Hunger is a rotten guest.
It swings from rib to rib like
a child on the monkey bars,
each touch heavy as a hammer,
the shock pulsing through the skull like
an earthquake in the dead of night.

I invite hunger in because
I was taught to be polite.
I know how to apply lipstick to a smile that is
not quite my own and to press wrinkles
from my dress—two sizes too small
to encourage hunger's presence—
knowledge gleaned from
the glossy pages of magazines
consumed during my springtime years.

Hunger makes me.
I was taught to martyr myself and
without hunger, I have nothing but
a body and a brain and
a new hunger, one which sits up,
and looks around,
and asks: "What now?"

Coming of Age

When I was eighteen, I learned to be
complicit in my own powerlessness. My
courage was not a small coal that I kept
swallowing, but rather a razor blade that
distanced me from the pain of
promises that never panned out. I learned that
time is not linear, that the past and present can
intersect, that then and now can
feel exactly the same. I
vomited cherry wine for a week, trying to
purge his touch from my skin from the
inside out, like exorcising the
vestiges of a bad dream. I hid the
skeleton of my former self in my closet and
left her to languish, because when I was
eighteen, I learned that entitled ears hear the
silence of a girl who is unconscious and
confuse it for the sound of consent.

You will not find love in the dictionary

You will not find love in the dictionary,
at a coffee shop, or in a church—
love is the thing that grows
    at the side of the curb,
an invasive species that
    refuses to be beaten down. It is
the wilted velvet of a week-old carnation
    abandoned on the porch,
the anger of a slamming door,
the lightning bolt of unexpected touch, and
the tumult of being arrested on
    the basis of undisclosed charges.
"Love" lives with me like
    a beetle under my skin,
traversing my veins like tunnels,
its scuttling legs louder than the bombs,
louder than the blood between my ears,
louder than the drop of
    a book in a barren room.
I once looked up love in the dictionary and
found only violence and the advice
    "take what you can get."

#Disconnected

When you and I were in free-fall
in the space between
what you said and what you meant,
I thought about the time you confessed
your dreams had outgrown your luggage.

I don't want to be the receptacle
from which you overflow, but
I still have hope smeared on my chest
in glow-in-the dark paint that I applied
in the space between
what you meant and what I heard.

Resilience is not a spot in the dark

Resilience is not a spot in the dark, and my
parchment-patched wings are more
sturdy than the sturdiest of walls. My
body is the home of a relentless flame, a
flicker that flares brightest under the
deep, deep sea, and my
spine is a trellis for the flowers that grow,
rootless, and the weeds that
crawl alongside them, unseen.

Ode to a False Deity

I am more than hopelessly devoted:
I am awake at dawn and dusk,
waiting, always waiting,
for the dust to settle,
my hungering body curled
at the base of your shrine,
my thoughts paper planes
made from newspapers
one day old, two days, three.

I am more than hopelessly devoted:
I will light myself on fire to
appease the gods, and
the mirror will never tell me
that I have burned enough, even after
my skin bubbles black
and falls from my bones
like the peel of a rotten banana.

I am not hopelessly devoted:
I am only afraid of what will happen
when I put down the knife
that keeps me away from myself.
I run on the fumes from our honeymoon,
fed by the memories of a decade past,
reaching through the fog for some relic
from when denial was power
and my hands didn't shake.

Hospital Poems

1. I landed in someone else's story,
an alien object yet to be identified.
I only occasionally fly—mostly,
I limp, hunched like walking with
a wound to the abdomen. Even more,
I wait, breath held, for things to happen,
for someone to find me and
yell it out like a game of charades.

2. I came to this dimension not
through the looking glass, but rather
through a pair of soft hands
caressing my skin while I
lay in the twilight zone of non-wakefulness,
the heat of sweet murmurs in my ear.

3. I know now I am other, but
other than what, I could not say.
They took my body to the shop
while I wasn't looking and in return
gave me voices that were not my own.
I hear indistinct whispers like a snake
slithering through the long, dry grass,
gossiping all day long.

4. There is a colony under my skin.
It writhes like something alive,
a cloud of wasps that stings from inside.
I must contain it, must find some equilibrium,
before it oozes like an oil spill.

5. Four walls: three shades of blue;
two tethers and one mirror, and
zero listening ears, although
an omniscient eye sits in the corner.
All night, I look in the mirror and I wonder
who looks back, and if they find me
interesting enough to keep.

6. I am a coffee table,
a fixture with a clear place and function.
My legs, once sturdy, now
groan and whimper like the slats of
a weather-worn bridge, serviceable but tenuous.
Here is a joke about coffee tables:
coffee tables should be seen and not heard.

The Easiest Way to Time Travel

You do not need a fancy machine
Or a wish in a well
Or magic potion
To take you back in time

All you require is your feet
Planted in your parents' kitchen
And the counters will suddenly seem
Ten feet taller than you ever will be

You are an actor in an absurdist play,
The tinnitus of a prepared piano
Ringing in your ears,
Constantly running the risk of ruin

As you are, as a ghost,
A spectre of childhoods past and potential,
You realize every time:
There truly is no place like home

Death and the Maiden

I put myself in a box under my bed.
It made me hard to love, but
I said I preferred it that way.

I cast pieces of myself out to sea
and wallpapered my house with
the bits that came back to me,
mutated and strange.

My life is like white elephants, where
order is a surrogate for connection.
If I believe hard enough,
one day it might come true.

The Song of Loneliness

When you swallow loneliness before it can
eat you alive, it opens a ravine in your soul,
deeper than the roots of the oldest tree.
A fire grows in that chasm, raw and insatiable,
a cold blue flame that burns through days like
a searchlight through the fog. It
hangs on with a terrier's tenacity,
teeth embedded in your heart as it
eclipses your stomach, the taste of carelessness
a distant memory, the ache comfortingly familiar,
like the soothing wash of a mother's lullaby.
It consumes you from the inside,
vicious and constant in its quest for connection,
a hollow thrum that is easily mistaken for
the thrill of life lived to the fullest by girls who
spend their years waiting for time to begin.

Recovery

I stood at the base of the spiral stairs
And stared up into the light

As I climbed I recited fridge magnet stories to myself
And to the shadows tattooed on the wall
And they danced with me as I
Reconstructed misguided histories

At the end, I realized that
Not all doors can be burned
Although they may be locked
And the key laid in earth

It is always a slippery slope
When your fingertips tingle with memory

Paperclip City

I am a goddess
    built from mosaics,

my paperclip ribs shielding
    my paper-mâché heart,

my lungs the wheels that spin
    breath into stories, and those stories

the foundation of my life and
    those whom I love.

I am not always strong in
    the broken places, but

where I am weak,
    I am wise, and

my wisdom is a collage of
    the kindness of strangers,

reminding me that the future is
    a chrysalis waiting to hatch.

Leftover Women

Sit with me another day? -

in the square where I lost a rib,
on the bench where They gather,

the "leftover women,"

shaken from their roosts like
dandelion dandruff gone to seed.

Transfiguration

I no longer speak the language of sacrifice: rather,
   sacrifice is a beast I grab by the skin of the neck,
   the man-made monster under the bed
   on which I shine a light.

I used to line my living room with
   dainty faces I kept in jars, but
   martyrdom is a bedrock on which
   I refuse to stand.

Find me guilty if you like:
   find me bossy
   and brusque
   and dramatic, but

I am not a lost-and-found
   or a library deposit box
   or the last suitcase
   left on the airport carousel, and

I no longer ship packages
   only to pray they get lost in the mail.

My heart is a moth in a glass jar

My heart is a moth in a glass jar,
my paper skin loose like drifting snow.
The ivy that binds me finds me

fingers outstretched to poke the
bear that is dawn, my reservoir the
sea where the gravestones lie.

I hoard my unspent life

I hoard my unspent life like
waiting for a rainy day
that never comes, and
I hold the unspeakable in my palms, though
mostly they stay in my pockets.
Every freeze-framed version of me
plays behind my split-screen eyelids as
I hurry to stay up-to-date
on my own current events. And yet,

when I collapse on the couch,
a cloud of butterflies erupts and
settles like dust, so close
I feel their wingbeats like heartbeats.
Despite pain, the most
patient teacher I ever had,
I still keep the last breath of summer
in my locket, cutting on
the borderline between the seasons
and catching rainbows when I can.

Balcony-Garden

I am a lookout
for the small things,
the stripes of light patterned
on an unmade bed
at the lazy wake of dawn,
the small, quiet intimacies
that go unremarked upon;
I hunt for the peace
of the things that I know
from the inside out,
an effort to un-destroy myself,
every freeze-framed version of me
stacked like records on a shelf,
while the stems
of my balcony-garden grow tall.

Skydiving

There are many ways to mature:
Softly and intentionally like
placing an egg in a basket, or in
starts and plateaus like the
rise of a grand staircase.

I unhooked my harness and
launched myself from the nest. I did not
aim to go gentle into that good night:
I was a comet overburdened with ambition.

I need a stake to keep my
head from the clouds, or perhaps a
leash, a tether to keep me, like a
dog, from where I ought not to go.

The soil on which I rest,
rootless, is fertilized by my own
frail deeds, but still I turn my head, distracted.
It is only ever now, I think, while the past
coils inside of me. I will be
unwinding it for a lifetime.

www.ingramcontent.com/pod-product-compliance
Lightning Source LLC
LaVergne TN
LVHW012054070526
838201LV00083B/4714